The Story of the
La Brea Tar Pits

Smilodon fatalis, *better known as the saber-toothed cat*

DATE DUE

11/17			
10 30			
1-15			

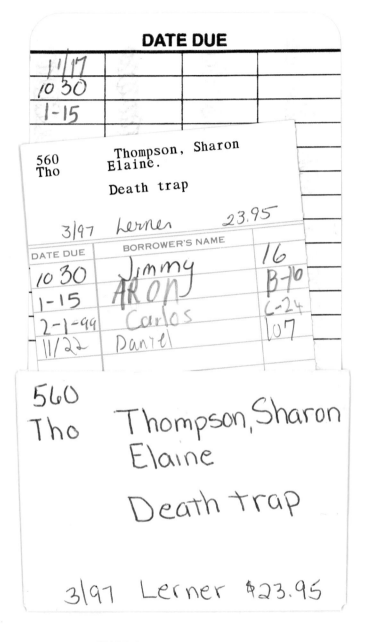

560
Tho

Thompson, Sharon
Elaine.

Death trap

3/97   Lerner   23.95

DATE DUE	BORROWER'S NAME	
10 30	Jimmy	16
1-15	ARON	B-10
2-1-99	Carlos	C-24
11/22	Daniel	L07

560
Tho

Thompson, Sharon
Elaine

Death trap

3/97 Lerner $23.95

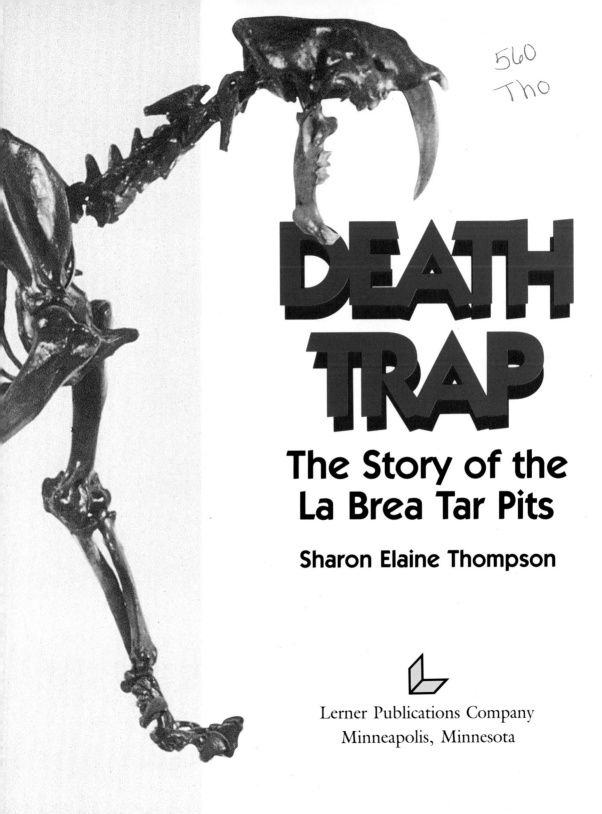

DEATH TRAP

The Story of the La Brea Tar Pits

Sharon Elaine Thompson

Lerner Publications Company
Minneapolis, Minnesota

With thanks to the staff members of the George C. Page Museum of La Brea Discoveries for their patience and humor. Special thanks to George Jefferson, Christopher Shaw, Shelley Cox, Eric Scott, Ellen Girardeau, James P. Quinn, and Fred Heald, who gave so generously of their time.

For my friend, H. David Morrow
Good things truly do come in small packages

Copyright © 1995 by Lerner Publications Company

Library of Congress Cataloging-in-Publication Data

Thompson, Sharon Elaine, 1952–
    Death trap : the story of the La Brea Tar Pits / Sharon Elaine Thompson.
        p. cm.
    Includes index.
    ISBN 0-8225-2851-7
    1. Paleontology—Pleistocene—Juvenile literature. 2. Fossils—California—La Brea Pits—Juvenile literature. 3. La Brea Pits (Calif.)—Juvenile literature. [1. Paleontology. 2. Fossils—California—La Brea Pits. 3. La Brea Pits (Calif.)].
    I. Title.
    QE741.2.T49 1995
    560'.178—dc20   93-39583
                                                      CIP
                                                      AC

Manufactured in the United States of America
    1 2 3 4 5 6 – I/JR – 99 98 97 96 95 94

CONTENTS

Sculptures aren't all we have to remind us of the mammoths that once roamed Los Angeles. We can also look at their bones!

INTRODUCTION

L os Angeles, California, is one of the world's busiest cities, and Wilshire Boulevard is one of its busiest streets. Cars and trucks rumble along, brakes screaming, horns blaring. Smog often fills the hot air.

Located along Wilshire Boulevard is Hancock Park. On the grass, kids throw Frisbees and play touch football. Nearby, school groups visit the art museum. At one corner of the park, right next to the street and sidewalk, there is a large, shiny, black pool.

Grasses growing around the pool are smeared and stained with oil. Near the edge of the pool, chest deep in water, stands a sculpture of an ancient elephant, a Columbian mammoth. Its trunk is up. It looks as if it is screaming in terror. Bubbles rise slowly to the surface of the water and burst. It seems as if something—or someone—is trapped at the bottom of the pond.

The smell of hot asphalt rises from the pool, an aroma that seems out of place in a sunny park. But 23-acre Hancock Park is no ordinary park. It is the site of the world-famous Rancho La Brea Tar Pits. Rancho La Brea (which means "tar ranch" in Spanish) is famous because of the millions of bones of Ice Age animals that have been found there—animals that, tens of thousands of years ago, were caught in a hidden, black death trap.

Just a few of the millions of bones unearthed at La Brea

Wells reaching thousands of feet into the ground allow people to tap the earth's petroleum deposits for fuel and other uses.

8

CHAPTER
1

THE MAKING OF A DEATH TRAP

Many of the bones at La Brea have lain buried in the tar pits for as long as 38,000 years. But the story of La Brea actually starts about 25 million years ago, during a time in the earth's history called the Miocene epoch. During the Miocene, conditions around what is now Hancock Park were just right for the formation of a liquid called petroleum, commonly known as oil. Asphalt, also called tar, comes from petroleum.

Petroleum is formed beneath the earth's surface by a slow, complicated process. The first ingredients in the creation of petroleum are living organisms—plants and animals.

All living things are organic—that is, they contain carbon, the same element found in charcoal and pencil leads. It is the carbon in plants and animals, primarily those that live in the ocean, that sometimes turns into oil.

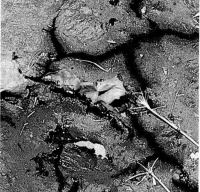

Oil still seeps to the earth's surface in Hancock Park, trapping leaves and branches—and sometimes even people!

A Recipe for Oil

The conversion of living things into oil starts when organisms die. Normally when plants and animals die, the carbon in them slowly combines with oxygen in the air or water to produce carbon dioxide gas. This action is part of the process we call decomposition, or decay.

Without enough oxygen, however, dead organisms cannot decay. Plant and animal remains may be cut off from oxygen if they are covered by mud or sand shortly after death. When this happens, the carbon in the organisms is trapped in the earth—and may eventually turn into oil.

The organisms that provided most of the carbon for oil formation at La Brea were plankton—microscopic marine (ocean-dwelling) plants and animals. When plankton die, they drift to the ocean floor, where they often decompose or are eaten by fish or other marine animals. Sometimes, however, dead plankton are covered by layers of sand and mud, or sediment. They are cut off from oxygen and don't decay.

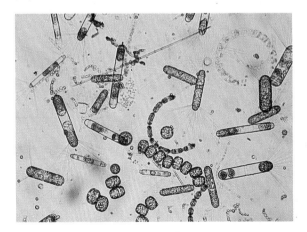

Plankton are tiny plants and animals that live in the sea. These are phytoplankton, microscopic plants.

10

As more sediment washes into the sea and settles on the ocean floor, the dead plankton are buried deeper. Over time the plankton may be buried under as much as five miles of sediment.

The weight of the sediment above squeezes water out of the layers below. Particles of sand and mud become packed very closely together, and chemical processes in the sediment glue the tiny particles into one large mass of rock. Because the rock is formed from sediment, we call it sedimentary rock. Layers of dead plankton are trapped inside it.

Time and Temperature Are All It Takes

As the rock is pressed deeper into the ground by tons of new sediment filtering down through the ocean, it becomes hotter. The increase in temperature is partly due to the pressure of the overlying rock and sediment. But it is also due to heat coming from molten, or melted, rock deeper inside the earth.

When the rock and dead plankton have been pushed into the earth to a depth of more than 8,000 feet (1½ miles), temperatures are high enough (175° to 275° Fahrenheit) to begin changing the carbon in the plankton to oil. Carbon does not turn to oil overnight, however. The conversion may take from 5 million to 50 million years!

Once it forms, oil may be trapped underground by impermeable rock—rock that does not allow liquid to pass through it. The oil may eventually leak out of the ground, however, to form asphalt traps, such as those at La Brea.

La Brea during the Miocene

The conditions at Rancho La Brea during the Miocene epoch were perfect for the formation of oil. The area that is now Hancock Park was then covered by the Pacific Ocean, which was filled with countless numbers of tiny plankton. And deep under the water, the earth was undergoing changes that would help form the La Brea oil deposits.

The earth's outer layer, or crust, is made up of enormous plates of rock. These plates move slowly across a layer of softer rock deep in the earth. The plates sometimes grind against or shove into each other. One of these plates is underneath the Pacific Ocean. Another carries the North American continent. In the early Miocene, about 18 million years ago, these two huge plates came into contact at the west coast of North America. The Pacific plate, which was moving north, ground against the North American plate.

This slow grinding movement caused changes in the ocean floor. In some areas, ridges formed. Underneath La Brea, however, the ocean floor began to subside, or sink. Over millions of years, the sea floor sank deeper, forming a huge basin, or underwater valley. There was little oxygen in the water near the bottom of the basin. A thick layer of undecayed plankton built up on the ocean floor.

Later in the Miocene, the North American plate, which was moving west, shoved into the Pacific plate. The land north of La Brea began to ripple, like a throw rug bunched up at one side. Rocks and soil were slowly pushed upward, creating mountains.

Rain, rivers, and streams washed sand and rock down the slopes of the slowly growing mountains into the ocean basin. For millions of years, sediment from the land buried dead plankton on the ocean floor. Pressed thousands of feet into the earth, the plankton began to turn into oil.

Sediment from the land continued to fill the basin. But another change was taking place on earth that would help turn the underwater valley into land. This change was the beginning of an ice age.

12

The Receding Sea

The earth has gone through several ice ages—periods when temperatures are very low and much of the land is covered with ice. During an ice age, rain often freezes, falling from the sky in the form of ice or snow. While some of this ice and snow melts, a lot of it remains frozen. It settles in ice sheets called glaciers, which spread out and cover great areas of land. So much of the earth's water is frozen in glaciers that less water is free to flow into the oceans. Gradually, the sea level drops. Land once covered by water becomes dry.

The most recent series of ice ages, which together are called the Great Ice Age, started about 2.5 million years ago. As the ocean receded, or moved back, from the mountains of California, the ocean basin that would become Hancock Park became shallower. Sediment continued to wash into the ocean basin— filling it in. Eventually the basin became land. Geologists, scientists who study the history of the earth, estimate that the area around Hancock Park has been a dry land valley for about 100,000 years.

Meanwhile, deep inside the earth, layers of sediment and dead plankton were turning into layers of rock and trapped oil—like alternating layers of cake and icing. As the North American and Pacific plates continued to push together, these layers were turned sideways, much like a layer cake standing on its side. Once the layers were on edge, the oil could flow out from between the rocks that trapped it. The great pressure deep in the earth pushed the oil upward—like a tube of toothpaste squeezed at the bottom. About 40,000 years ago, oil began to flow upward and seep, or leak out, through the loose sand and gravel at La Brea.

MIOCENE EPOCH			PLIOCENE EPOCH	
25 million years ago	18 million years ago	5 million years ago	1.7 million years ago	
	North American and Pacific plates collide	Underwater basin and ridges form at La Brea	Oil begins to form beneath ocean floor	Ocean begins to recede

Traps Underfoot

Oil, or petroleum, is made up of many kinds of hydrocarbons, including gasoline and kerosene. Some of the hydrocarbons in petroleum evaporate—change from liquid into gas—very quickly when they come into contact with air. When these hydrocarbons evaporate, they leave behind a thick, sticky, black substance called asphalt. Asphalt is commonly, although incorrectly, called tar.

Because oil seeps to the surface of the earth, deposits such as those at La Brea are called asphalt seeps. La Brea is not the only asphalt seep in the world. Asphalt deposits may be found wherever oil is found.

During winter, asphalt in seeps is hard, just like the asphalt we use to pave streets. But in the warmth of summer, asphalt becomes soft and sticky. It flows into low spots in the ground or settles into streambeds or ponds. Dirt and leaves cling to it. Water and sand cover it. The asphalt becomes a trap for anything that steps into it.

Asphalt-filled depressions once covered many acres around La Brea. For thousands of years, many of the animals that wandered through the area were trapped in the tar.

14

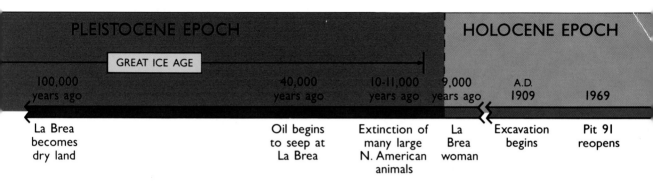

PLEISTOCENE EPOCH				HOLOCENE EPOCH	

GREAT ICE AGE

100,000 years ago	40,000 years ago	10-11,000 years ago	9,000 years ago	A.D. 1909	1969
La Brea becomes dry land	Oil begins to seep at La Brea	Extinction of many large N. American animals	La Brea woman	Excavation begins	Pit 91 reopens

This diagram shows oil escaping to the earth's surface through layers of rock and sediment.

15

Mammoths, giant sloths, camels, and a host of other creatures once lived in southern California.

CHAPTER
2

PREHISTORIC LIFE AT LA BREA

The area around Los Angeles, California, is now a scrubby semidesert, hot and dry in summer, riverbeds empty of water. In winter the region is cool and rainy. But the rain often falls too quickly to be absorbed by the soil. Instead, a lot of the water rushes into rivers and streams and off to the ocean. Low, drought-resistant shrubs called chaparral grow throughout the region. But because water is often scarce, large trees are not common in the natural landscape around Los Angeles.

Los Angeles was much different 40,000 years ago, however. When the oil of La Brea first began to seep from the ground, the earth was close to the end of a time period called the Pleistocene epoch, which started about 1.7 million years ago and ended about 10,000 years ago. During much of the Pleistocene, the earth was in the grip of the Great Ice Age. More than 28 percent of the land on earth

Glaciers like this one once covered vast areas of land.

was covered with ice (compared to about 10 percent today). In North America, glaciers stretched from the Arctic Ocean to present-day St. Louis, Missouri.

Although there were no glaciers in southern California during the Pleistocene, average temperatures were about 10°F lower than they are today, and the weather was much wetter. Hancock Park was crisscrossed by streams and dotted with small ponds. The moisture and lower temperatures enabled trees such as oaks and pines to grow in the valley. Enormous redwoods grew in the nearby mountains. But there were also areas of open plain.

Not only the plants of La Brea were different tens of thousands of years ago. The animals were different too. Southern California was home to huge, cold-weather animals—many of which are now extinct. Ancient elephants, such as mammoths and mastodons, played and wallowed in the pools and streams. Some of these elephants were 13 feet tall and weighed 10 tons. Giant ground sloths, taller than a human, roamed the valley, browsing on trees and shrubs. Ancient bison—often called buffalo—migrated into the region every year. Herds of horses and even an occasional camel came to the pools to drink.

Most of the large animals of the valley were plant-eaters, or herbivores. They were bound to attract carnivores, meat-eaters such as dire wolves, American lions, and saber-toothed cats, which stalked through the trees and across the plains hunting for food.

A Feast in the Asphalt

Occasionally, predators (the hunters) found their prey (the hunted) trapped in water holes and streams. Large, heavy herbivores, stepping up to the water to drink, could become stuck in asphalt hidden by water, dirt, or rotten leaves. Finding themselves trapped and unable to move, the terrified animals screamed and

18

An artist's recreation of an entrapment episode as it might have occurred 35,000 years ago

fought to get free. Their cries only let predators, always ready for an easy meal, know that they were in trouble.

The carnivores, however, found that this meal was not so easy. As they waded into the water themselves, or circled a trapped animal, their paws became stuck in the asphalt. Their angry snarls alerted still more predators.

Even meat-eating birds often could not escape entrapment. As they swooped to their meal and settled on the dying and dead animals, their wing feathers sometimes dipped in the asphalt, making them unable to fly. These birds, too, became part of the feast.

These animals did not sink out of sight in deep lakes of tar, however. Although today we refer to the deposits at La Brea as "tar pits," the original deposits were not lakes or even ponds. They were more like large puddles, perhaps only a few inches deep. Although it may be hard to believe that such shallow deposits could have trapped enormous animals, they did. Two inches of asphalt will snare modern cattle that are unlucky enough to wander into an asphalt seep.

Because the asphalt deposits were very shallow, dead animals might lie on the surface for months. Scavengers—animals, such as coyotes, that eat dead animals—were the next visitors to the site. Those scavengers that were fortunate enough to escape with only sticky paws sometimes pulled bones from the asphalt, fought over them, dragged them away from the kill site, and picked them clean of meat. Loose bones might decay for a while. Later, a new flow of asphalt might bury them. Or spring rains might wash the bones into a stream and carry them to another asphalt seep.

More oil oozed up from the ground, depositing more asphalt around the bones. Dirt, twigs, and leaves gradually covered and buried them. Everything would be quiet again—until another animal blundered into the tar.

This series of events—from the trapping of an herbivore until the last scavenger has left the site—is called an entrapment episode. Paleontologists, scientists who study life from the past, used to think that animals were caught in the asphalt every day. But now they believe that this kind of prehistoric drama did not happen every day, every week, or even every year. Scientists estimate that large entrapment episodes might have happened only once every ten years or so. Each episode involved dozens of animals.

Scientists think that the entrapment of a large herbivore usually started the episode. But most of the animals (90 percent

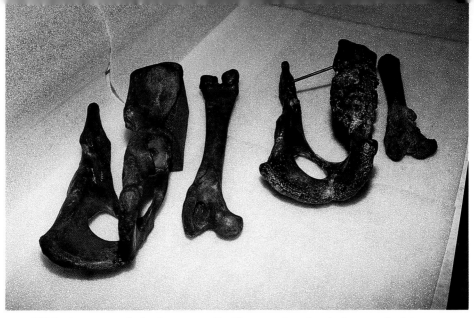

Oil has preserved the bones at La Brea and stained them a dark coffee color.

of the mammals and 70 percent of the birds) caught in the asphalt at La Brea were predators and scavengers. For every large herbivore found in the asphalt, scientists have found one saber-toothed cat, one coyote, and four dire wolves.

Predators and scavengers outnumber herbivores at La Brea because predators hunt and eat any animal that is weak or dying. Scavengers eat any dead animal—whether it is predator or prey. As predators and scavengers got caught trying to eat the trapped herbivores, they often became food for other meat-eaters.

The bones of these prehistoric victims of the asphalt have lain buried for thousands of years. Most of them have not decomposed, however. Bones are porous, meaning they contain microscopic holes that allow liquid to flow through them. As the ancient animal bones lay in the asphalt, oil saturated, or filled, them completely. The oil pushed all air and oxygen out of the bones, preventing decomposition and thus preserving them. The bones have become fossils.

A shell turned to stone

From Animal to Fossil

Fossils are remains of or evidence of past life on earth. A fossil may be a shell that has turned to stone, a dinosaur footprint in mud that has turned to rock, or bones preserved in asphalt. Dead insects trapped in amber (the resin of ancient trees) and the frozen remains of extinct Siberian elephants are also considered fossils.

Most fossils come from the hard parts of animals, such as shells or bones. Usually, the soft parts—muscles, skin, and organs—are quickly attacked by bacteria when the animal dies, and they decay. Plant parts, such as leaves, seeds, and wood, can also become fossils.

For a plant or animal to fossilize, the organism must be buried quickly so it won't decay. The chemical conditions must also be right. Sometimes chemicals in the ground slowly dissolve buried bones, shells, or plants. Minerals then replace the dissolved organism, creating a stone duplicate of the original. Sometimes a hollow spot left when an organism dissolves is not filled. This hole in the rock, in the shape of an ancient plant or animal, is also a fossil.

The fossils of La Brea are unique. Most fossils have been altered or changed in some way—turned to stone, for example. Other fossils are only the traces of an ancient organism, such as the outline of a leaf left in rock. But the bones in the asphalt at La Brea are still bones. Although they are filled with oil, they are pretty much the same as they would be if the animals had died only yesterday. Seeds found at La Brea are unchanged from the day they fell from the plants of the Pleistocene. Insect skeletons and snail shells, too, are unchanged.

The fossils of La Brea lay in the ground for a long time before they were discovered by humans. It was even longer before humans began to understand how important the bones were and to collect them.

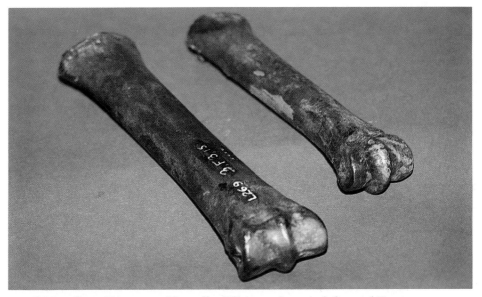

Bones from Equus occidentalis *(Western horse),* left, *and* Equus conversidens *(Mexican horse), both now extinct*

The La Brea dig begins.

24

CHAPTER

3

EXCAVATING A TOMB
OF TAR

People have lived in California for thousands of years. The first Californians used the asphalt reserves at La Brea and probably knew about the bones there. Later, Spanish settlers noticed the asphalt deposits and the fossils in them. But it wasn't until the early 20th century that scientists became interested in La Brea's fossils and the tales the bones had to tell.

The first written report of the La Brea asphalt was made in 1769 by Father Juan Crespi. Crespi was traveling from Mexico to Monterey, California, with Gaspar de Portolá, the newly appointed Spanish governor of California. In his journal, Crespi recorded passing "swamps of bitumen [asphalt]" as he rode north. He and Portolá thought that the seeping asphalt might have caused an earthquake that they had felt a few days before.

In 1792 José Longinos Martinez, another Spanish visitor to the area, wrote about seeing unlucky creatures trapped in asphalt, as well as bones that had come up to the surface. "After many years," he wrote about the trapped animals, "their bones have come up through holes, as if petrified [turned to stone]." He did not realize that the bones he saw were from ancient animals, not modern ones. For the next 80 years, no one else realized it either.

By 1870 California had become part of the United States, and much of the land around the tar pits was owned by Major Henry Hancock. In 1875 geologist William Denton, a member of the Boston Society of Natural History, visited Hancock at his ranch. Hancock gave Denton an animal's tooth he had found on his property, and Denton recognized it to be a canine tooth from the extinct saber-toothed cat. Denton was the first person to write in scientific journals about the fossilized bones at La Brea.

Twentieth-Century Bone Rush

Denton's report did not create much scientific excitement. In fact, it was apparently overlooked or ignored. Then, 25 years later, bones of other extinct animals were discovered when a well was drilled on the Hancock property. Geologist W. W. Orcutt identified the bones, and scientists and amateur paleontologists took notice. The bone rush was on.

In the early 1900s, the deposits at La Brea were surrounded by farmland—not apartments, office buildings, and traffic. As one early collector recalled, "I'd catch the west bound [street]car out on 16th Street and get off several hours later at a little flag stop out in the grain fields. I would walk...for about three-quarters of a mile till I got to the diggings."

The diggers found a wealth of fossils in the thick deposits. Although the puddles of asphalt that had trapped the ancient animals had been shallow, over the course of 40,000 years, layers of asphalt, fossils, soil, and debris had built up in and around the deposits. By the time fossil hunters arrived, the deposits were many feet deep.

In one deposit, at a depth of 4 feet, diggers struck the top of a stump of an ancient tree. They found the roots of the tree another 8 feet down. In the thousands of years since the tree's roots had first been touched by tar, 12 feet of asphalt, sand, and soil had accumulated.

The first major controlled excavation of the La Brea deposits was started in 1909 by James Z. Gilbert and some of his students from Los Angeles High School. A few years later, their collection of fossils formed the core of the exhibit in the Museum of History, Science, and Art (later renamed the Natural History Museum of Los Angeles County).

In 1913 George Allan Hancock, Henry's son, gave the museum exclusive rights to dig at La Brea for two years. All the fossils found during that time were donated to the museum. While many deposits were empty of bones, more than 750,000 fossils were recovered from the pits during the excavation. In the two years, the museum staff excavated 96 asphalt deposits—Pit 1 through Pit 96. The resulting cone-shaped holes, which eventually filled with asphalt and water, gave the site its nickname: Tar Pits.

George Allan Hancock

W. W. Orcutt

Fossil recovery was not easy work, and sometimes it was dangerous. Some pits were 30 feet deep. Wall supports were inadequate, and pits frequently caved in. Black smoke sometimes hung over the field as workers burned liquid asphalt that had been removed from the deposits.

Every asphalt deposit was unique. Pit 13 contained the remains of mostly small animals. Pits 61 and 67 revealed human artifacts as well as bones of extinct animals. Pit 9 contained almost 95 percent of all the ancient elephant bones—those from mammoths and mastodons—found at Rancho La Brea. Researchers believe that the asphalt in Pit 9 may have bubbled up into a large, deep pool of water and that the elephants were snared when they came to the pool to wallow in the water and mud.

By the end of 1915, most of the 96 deposits had been completely excavated. Pit 91 was only about 10 feet deep, however, when the digging stopped. The pit was left open as an exhibit, and although it was supposed to be roofed over, a shelter was never built. Nor was the site maintained. Gradually, Pit 91 filled with asphalt and debris. For 54 years it was neglected.

Pit 91 Reopens

In 1969 workers from the Natural History Museum of Los Angeles County reopened Pit 91 and started digging where the previous excavation had stopped. Now, every summer, volunteers and staff from the Natural History Museum and the George C. Page Museum of La Brea Discoveries remove the asphaltic matrix (the asphalt-saturated sand and soil that surrounds the bones) and recover fossils from the pit. By 1993 the excavation was about 14 feet deep, and paleontologists expected to remove another 5 to 7 feet of asphalt and bones to find the earliest fossils—trapped in the deposit perhaps 35,000 years ago.

Pit 91 is the site of a systematic, although messy, excavation.

This drawer, one of thousands at the Page Museum, holds nothing but coyote teeth.

Scientists and volunteers work at the excavation only two months each summer—when the asphalt is warm and easiest to remove. Another reason the digging season is so short, explains paleontologist George Jefferson, is that if the dig were worked year-round, the huge numbers of fossils removed from the asphalt would overwhelm the museum's storage facilities. The Page Museum, which is adjacent to the asphalt deposits, already houses an estimated three million individual fossil specimens, says collections manager Christopher Shaw.

Slow, Dirty Work

The techniques used at the excavation site today have changed significantly from the system designed for the excavation in 1913. The process is safer than it was 80 years ago, and the record-keeping system is much more accurate. But the work is still not very glamorous.

Pit 91 is about 28 feet square, its walls supported by steel beams and lined with tar-stained boards. A thin layer of asphalt continually covers the floor of the pit and seeps up the steel beams. Volunteers wearing tar-splattered T-shirts and jeans remove approximately 80 gallons of excess asphalt a week in a procedure they call "glopping." They use trowels, or small shovels, to scrape asphalt from the floor of the excavation. They "glop" it into buckets and haul it up to the surface. Then they dump it into another nearby asphalt deposit, "where it's probably recycled right back into the pit," jokes paleontologist Eric Scott.

The only spots of color in the oil-stained pit are the orange hard hats worn by staff and volunteers and the bright yellow nylon cord crisscrossing the bottom. The cord, just inches from the floor, divides the pit into a grid of 3-foot by 3-foot squares. Workers excavate each square to a depth of 6 inches. They finish all the squares on each 6-inch level before going on to the level below.

Before a fossil is removed from the asphalt, diggers photograph and sketch it while it is still in place. They also note each fossil's location by measuring its distance from two sides of the grid and its depth in the 6-inch level. Later, workers will enter these measurements into a computer, which will create a three-dimensional diagram showing exactly how each bone was positioned in the mass. This diagram will help scientists understand how the asphalt deposit formed.

Excavators must be careful not to damage the fossils as they're working. Having been buried for 10,000 to 40,000 years, the bones have become fragile and can easily break. Workers must also avoid scarring the surface of the fossils. Scientists will study these surfaces to learn how an animal died, how its muscles were attached to the bone, and whether or not it was the victim of disease.

To remove the fossils, excavators kneel and sit on boards laid on the asphalt. They work carefully to remove each bone from the matrix, using tools such as small chisels, dental picks, and soft brushes. Large fossils, like the skull of a saber-toothed cat, might take days to remove. Because the diggers work so carefully and

"Glopping" tar

32

Workers remove fossils from the asphalt with extreme care. They put tiny specimens inside gelatin capsules for protection.

slowly, excavating a single grid square can take between three days and two months. And because they dig just two months per year, excavating an entire 6-inch level may take several years.

Although the excavation work is slow and painstaking, paleontologists at La Brea admit that they are spoiled by the relative ease with which they can remove fossils from the deposit. Paleontologists working at other kinds of fossil sites use drills, large chisels, hammers, and acids to free specimens from soil and rock. At La Brea, the asphaltic matrix is comparatively soft and easy to remove from the bones.

Tiny Clues and Missing Pieces

When paleontologists started excavating the fossils in the early 1900s, they were mostly interested in large, showy, museum-quality specimens. They rarely saved bones from animals smaller than a rabbit. Yet very few of the specimens found in the La Brea deposits—less than 1 percent—belong to large animals, says Christopher Shaw. In fact, he explains, for every large bone found, there are 200 to 500 more fossils that belong to small animals and plants.

Today workers retrieve all the fossils, regardless of size. As a result of this work, paleontologists have added more than 350 species to the list of plants and animals known to have lived in the Los Angeles area during the late Pleistocene—bringing the total number of known species to 625. The fossils recovered at La Brea make up the most well-documented collection of ancient terrestrial (land-dwelling) life in the world.

Microfossils are just as important to researchers as big bones.

In addition to digging up bones, workers remove and save several buckets of asphalt from each square of the grid. Later, they will dissolve the asphalt to find microfossils—tiny bones, seeds, snail shells, and insect shells. Even microscopic one-celled plants have been removed from the asphalt.

The tar pits do not contain the remains of all the species of animals that lived at La Brea during the Pleistocene, however. Some types of animals living in the area may never have been caught in the tar. Others may have been caught so rarely that only a few of their bones have been found. Some animal remains are not preserved by asphalt at all. Claws, beaks, hooves, feathers, skin, and hair, for instance, are made up of a material called keratin, which decomposes in asphalt.

Pitfalls of Urban Excavation

La Brea is not the only asphalt seep being excavated for fossils. There are three similar sites in California as well as one in Peru. But the fossil excavation at La Brea is the only one of its kind taking place in the heart of a major city. The site's location creates a whole set of special problems for paleontologists.

The Ice Age asphalt deposits cover an area much larger than the 23 acres of Hancock Park. So, occasionally, when new buildings go up or old ones are torn down in neighborhoods near the park, new fossil-bearing asphalt deposits are found. When this happens, scientists have to act very quickly. They have no time for careful excavation when the bulldozers are standing by. They simply salvage what they can.

One such deposit was found in the early 1990s during construction of a new apartment building. Paleontologists and volunteers removed the first 8 feet of asphalt, which was packed with thousands of bird bones, and stored it in 150 5-gallon buckets.

The remainder of the deposit was left in the ground. Perhaps it will be excavated someday in the future, when the building that is new today comes down to be replaced.

Another deposit, uncovered in 1975 when the Page Museum was built, had formed very differently from the others at Rancho La Brea. It was flat, not deep and cone-shaped like the typical asphalt deposit, and it was only 1½- to 2½-feet thick. Scientists believe that the asphalt there had flowed down a slope into a depression created by a shallow pool of water. The asphalt had probably seeped to the surface at a different place.

Because of this deposit's size and shape, workers were able to remove it all. They split the deposit into 20 large blocks, wrapped them in newspapers, and packed them into plaster-saturated burlap for protection. One by one, the blocks are being excavated in the Page Museum laboratory.

Indoor Excavation

One of the plaster-encased blocks, roughly 4 feet by 3 feet by 2 feet, sits in the middle of the lab. The top has been sliced off. Poking through the surface are the broken ribs of a saber-toothed cat and the claw and partial skeleton of an eagle. Other secrets remain hidden in the asphalt.

Out in Pit 91, excavators take measurements by hand, with rulers. But the procedure in the lab more closely resembles a hospital operating room. A metal frame is attached to the ceiling above the block of asphalt. Each corner of the frame holds a microphone. A computer sits close by.

Using an instrument called a sonic probe, a paleontologist touches the fossil she wants to measure. She presses a button, and the probe emits a series of clicks, which are picked up by the microphones. The computer analyzes the distance the sound

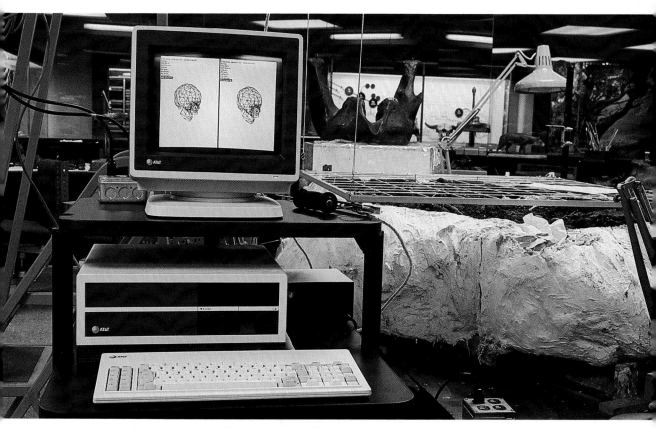

A sonic probe (sitting next to the monitor) and computer-generated graphics help scientists in the lab.

travels to each of the four mikes and then plots the exact position of the bone in the block.

After all the fossils have been measured and removed, the computer can then produce three-dimensional graphics showing the placement of every bone in the asphalt block. In effect, the scientists use the computer to pick the block up, turn it, and look at it from different angles.

Cleaning the Fossils

Whether they are excavated outside or inside, once the bones are out of the asphalt, they must be cleaned. Large specimens are cleaned by hand with a liquid called chloroethane, which dissolves asphalt and oil. Not all the oil is removed from the fossils, though, because oil preserves the bone. If all the oil were soaked out, the fossils would begin to decompose.

After they are cleaned, the fossils are coated with a fast-drying glue. This coating protects the fossils from moisture and keeps them from crumbling. As a bonus, the coating seals in the remaining oil, so the fossils don't stain museum displays.

At one time, the bucketsful of asphalt taken from each grid square in Pit 91 were boiled in chloroethane, to remove the asphalt and to make it easy for workers to retrieve tiny fossils. Then scientists discovered that chloroethane is toxic and can cause cancer. Los Angeles city officials decided that the fumes produced by the boiling process were too dangerous to be released into the atmosphere and that the sludge, the asphalt that remained after chloroethane treatment, could not be disposed of safely. Museum workers no longer use chloroethane to retrieve microfossils from the matrix. They are searching for other solvents that won't damage the fossils or the environment. In the meantime, the bucketsful of asphalt are being stored.

A Job for Patient People

Once cleaned, fossils are sorted, labeled, and pieced together in the lab. Most of the work is done by volunteers, ranging from high school juniors to retirees. The volunteers must have a great deal of patience. Inside the lab, one volunteer gently turns, twists, and tries to match together broken fragments of bone. A

A Natural History Museum staff member examines the reconstructed lower jaw of an American mastodon (Mammut americanum).

carefully reconstructed rib, systematically glued together, lies next to his elbow.

Nearby, another volunteer uses a magnifier to sort microfossils from Pit 91. The pile in front of her looks like coarse sand. Most of it is just that. But the volunteer's practiced hands and eyes effortlessly separate tiny freshwater shells, minute bones, fragments of insect carapaces (shells), and plant material from the sand.

Across the room, two teenage girls separate specimens from boxes of broken and unidentified bones dug up in the early 1900s. Some boxes contain a slip of paper, giving little information about the bones other than their pit number and collection date. The volunteers sort the fossils into separate piles of teeth, pieces of jaw, and a large pile of "I-don't-knows."

With all the new fossils workers are recovering from Pit 91, it hardly seems worth the trouble to clean 80 years of dust from these leftovers, but it is. Tucked away in the boxes, unnoticed for years, were the remains of a saber-toothed cat called *Homotherium* and a small, burro-sized horse. Before the old boxes were reexamined, scientists hadn't known that either species had lived west of the Rocky Mountains.

These are only a couple of the discoveries that scientists have made by taking another, closer look at old bones. Through their examination of the fossils of La Brea, paleontologists are gaining some vivid insights into life in the Hancock Park area at the end of the Pleistocene.

Many bones from the first dig at La Brea gathered dust for decades.

CHAPTER
4

A New Look
at Old Bones

In the late 1800s and early 1900s, paleontology was still a fairly new science. Paleontologists often competed to get the biggest and the best fossils for their museums. They commonly ignored small, broken, damaged, or abnormal bones. They rarely documented the way bones lay in a deposit. Early fossil hunters were usually more interested in the appearance of the bones they collected than the secrets locked in them.

Modern paleontologists, however, are taking a new look at old bones. They have found that plain, broken, and abnormal fossils can tell them a lot about the way ancient animals survived. Small microfossils give scientists information about the environment in which the animals lived. The way the bones lie in a deposit and how they are arranged with respect to each other can tell paleontologists about the way animals died. Today at La Brea, all fossils are collected and recorded with great care.

Perfectly Preserved

Because they are saturated by oil, fossils from La Brea are all a coffee-colored brown. Oil saturation also gives the fossils their most important characteristic: they are extremely well preserved. In fact,

A broken bone shows oil penetration to the very core.

except for the oil and brown coloration, the bones at La Brea might have come from animals that died yesterday.

Oil-saturated bones show all the detail of living bone, including marks where muscles were once attached and where blood vessels passed close by. Oil has penetrated to the very center of the bones—to the marrow, the spongy tissue at the core. In broken bones, the marrow is distinctly visible, each cell filled with oil. Even the animals' DNA is often preserved.

DNA, or deoxyribonucleic acid, is the material in living cells that determines each organism's hereditary traits. Scientists have been able to analyze DNA from the bones at La Brea to learn about animals that are now extinct. One of these animals is the saber-toothed cat. Until recently, scientists could not prove that saber-toothed cats were related to modern cats. But by examining DNA from La Brea's fossils, researchers have discovered that the ancient cat is indeed part of the family of big modern cats such as lions, tigers, and leopards.

How Old Is Old?

To find out how old the La Brea fossils are, paleontologists use a chemical clock that is built into every living thing. The element that runs this clock is radioactive carbon, or carbon 14.

All living things contain carbon 14. Plants absorb it from the atmosphere. Animals take in carbon 14 when they eat plants or when they eat other animals that have eaten plants. Carbon 14 is stored in tissues, such as bones. Although carbon 14 breaks down while it is inside plants and animals, organisms constantly take in more of it. While an organism lives, the amount of carbon 14 it contains remains constant.

When an organism dies, however, it stops taking in carbon 14. Over thousands of years, the carbon 14 in a dead organism decays and turns into nitrogen. As the amount of carbon 14 decreases, the amount of nitrogen increases.

Carbon 14 converts to nitrogen at a very steady, predictable rate. In 5,730 years, half of the carbon 14 in a dead organism will have changed into nitrogen. In another 5,730 years, half of the remaining carbon 14 will have changed to nitrogen, and so on. Scientists call this 5,730-year period the "half-life" of radioactive carbon.

By comparing the amount of carbon 14 to the amount of nitrogen in a fossil, scientists can tell how long the carbon 14 has been decaying and how long the organism has been dead. After about 40,000 to 50,000 years, the amount of radioactive carbon in a fossil is so small that it is difficult to measure. So carbon dating is not used to date fossils older than about 50,000 years.

DNA analysis cannot tell researchers anything about the Ice Age environment, though, or about extinct animals' behavior or social structure. Nor would scientists be able to get this information by looking at only a few sample fossils, no matter how well preserved. But the La Brea asphalt deposits are unique in the huge numbers of fossils discovered there. The storage rooms at the George C. Page Museum hold rows of 7-foot-tall cabinets filled with teeth, skulls, backbones, and leg bones—approximately 3 million individual specimens. By looking at so many fossils, scientists can begin to see patterns that give them insight into the behavior of many of the Pleistocene animals.

Cabinet after cabinet holds the vast collection at the Page Museum.

Wandering Bison

To learn about extinct bison (*Bison antiquus*), for instance, George Jefferson and other researchers examined the jaws and teeth of 288 of these animals. By noting how worn the teeth were, the scientists could tell how old the bison were when they died. Researchers noticed that the bison teeth found at La Brea belonged to animals that were about a year apart in age. There were many teeth from bison calves just over one year old and from calves just over two years old, for example.

This discovery told researchers that the bison were only at La Brea once a year. Jefferson explains that if the bison had lived in the region all year-round, the asphalt would have contained teeth from calves of all ages. Instead, the animals were migrating, moving from one area to another, in a yearly cycle. Each time the herd came to La Brea, some of the young animals died in the asphalt. (As many as two-thirds of the bones found at La Brea belong to subadult, or young, animals. Scientists think that young animals often were not strong enough to pull themselves from the tar, or that they did not have any experience with the tar that would have taught them to be cautious about it.)

The teeth even told scientists where the animals were migrating from, says Jefferson. When researchers examined the teeth under a microscope, they were surprised to find pieces of grass preserved in the tooth cavities. Grass fossils have not been discovered at La Brea. So researchers checked and learned that the grasses in the teeth all came from the edges of California's deserts. Therefore, Jefferson explains, the animals must have spent the wet winters in the desert areas and wandered into La Brea in late spring, when the deserts dried up. Neither he nor anyone else knows where the bison went when they left the tar pits, however.

Secrets of the Saber-Toothed Cat

Piecing together an animal's behavior from fossilized clues takes patience. Even then, not all paleontologists interpret the clues the same way. And their interpretations may change when new discoveries are made. At La Brea, scientists are constantly revising old theories.

For example, early scientists thought that saber-toothed cats used their sabers, their gigantic canine teeth, to bite into their prey's throat. But, explains Christopher Shaw, researchers now believe that by attacking the throat, a cat would have risked breaking a canine on the bones in its victim's neck. Breaking a tooth—its primary weapon—would have been disastrous for a cat. It would be unable to hunt and would probably starve.

Not only that, says Shaw, but if the saber-toothed cat did indeed bite the throat of its prey, the teeth found at La Brea would show signs of wear from constant contact with neck bones. However, none of these teeth show any unusual signs of wear. In fact, many of the teeth in the Page Museum collection are in nearly perfect condition. So modern researchers tend to believe that the saber-toothed cat struck at the soft belly of its prey, where there would be little risk of breaking its canines.

Another theory that has undergone revision was put forth by Chester Stock, an early La Brea paleontologist. Stock noticed that a number of saber-toothed cat bones at La Brea showed signs of injury. He theorized that injured cats came to the asphalt deposits to find a constant source of food—animals that were dead or dying in the tar.

But, as we learned earlier, scientists now believe that animals became trapped only once in a while at La Brea, in large entrapment episodes that might have been as much as 10 years apart.

Charles Knight made this painting of prehistoric La Brea in 1926.

While there might have been enough food for an injured saber-toothed cat to live on during an entrapment episode, not even one weak or injured cat could have found enough food at the asphalt to survive between episodes.

So why have so many damaged saber-toothed cat bones been found at La Brea? To learn the answer, let's take a look at the kinds of damage scientists have found. The first kind of injury comes from the everyday strain a hunting animal puts on its body. Whenever an animal strains or pulls ligaments (the fibers that hold bones together) the body responds by producing more bone to strengthen the weakened area. If the animal continues to strain the same area, the repeated injury shows up in the fossils as thickened spots on the bone.

In saber-toothed cats, paleontologists commonly see thickening in the bones the cats used every day to survive. Injured areas are found on the front legs—along the muscles used to rotate, or turn, the paws and wrists—and on the back legs—along the muscles the cat used to leap. The front and back ends of the ribs are also damaged, from the impact of the cat's chest crashing into its prey. Some neckbones and backbones had apparently been compressed (squeezed together) and twisted so often that the bones had grown together. All these injuries give scientists a picture of an active and efficient predator.

The pattern in the injuries also supports the theory that the cat stabbed its prey in the belly, not the throat. The following is the kind of drama scientists now believe might have taken place on the plains around La Brea more than 10,000 years ago.

The saber-toothed cat was larger than an African lion and powerfully built through the chest, shoulders, and front legs. After a short run, the cat would leap onto a young mammoth or other large prey, its chest slamming into the animal, the bones in its back compressing with the impact. The cat would then grapple with its prey, perhaps balancing on its hind legs while it fought. This balancing act caused the cat's lower back to twist as the prey struggled. With its powerful forelegs, the saber-toothed cat would then pull the victim over onto its back, exposing the animal's belly. Using its 8-inch-long sabers, the cat would open an enormous wound in the victim's side.

If the prey were a young mammoth, its mother might be coming to the rescue about this time. If the cat did not get out of the way quickly, it might be maimed or killed by the adult elephant. So the cat probably retreated, waiting for the young animal to die and for the mother to move off before going in to feed on its kill.

In such struggles with their prey, the cats were not always able to escape injury themselves. Victims often fought back by kicking, tossing, or stepping on the cats. Traumatic or severe injuries,

The pelvis and right femur (thighbone) of a saber-toothed cat show cartilage destruction and a massive inflammatory infection. How did the crippled cat survive?

such as broken or dislocated bones, are the second kind of damage seen in saber-toothed cats at La Brea. After a severe injury, a lot of extra bone will build up to strengthen a weakened area—far more bone than results from everyday wear. In fact, many bones in the collection at the Page Museum are badly misshapen as a result of the buildup.

Amazingly, massive injuries did not always kill the cats. Although undoubtedly in a great deal of pain, they often managed to heal and survive. By looking at the amount of everyday wear and tear that occurred *after* the bones were healed, scientists know that injured saber-toothed cats sometimes lived as long as two or three years before becoming mired in the asphalt at La Brea.

But how did injured animals survive while they were healing? To answer this questions, scientist have taken a look at modern cat families. Scientists think that the only way the crippled cats could have survived would have been by living in family groups, as do modern African lions. If that were the case, the injured cat would have been able to eat some of the meat caught and killed by other animals in the group. The cat might have been able to live long enough to heal and hunt again.

Telltale Claws

New discoveries at La Brea have revised theories not only about the saber-toothed cat's behavior but also about what the cat looked like. One such discovery changed paleontologists' ideas about the saber-toothed cat's claws.

Scientists recreate a skeleton for a museum by piecing together an animal's bones. But most of the La Brea deposits contained bones from all sorts of animals, all mixed together. As a result, skeletons at the Page Museum are constructed using bones from many individual animals of a single species.

One reconstructed saber-toothed cat's paw, for instance, was made up of bones taken from at least six different pits. The cats had immense paws, 6 to 7 inches across—almost as large as a dinner plate. Each paw was tipped by five huge claw sheaths, coverings that protected the claws when they were not being used and kept them sharp. Paleontologists thought that all the sheaths on a paw were the same size and that each would have held a huge claw.

But when the flat desposit was found during construction of the Page Museum, diggers found many animals whose bones were almost undisturbed—their skeletons more or less in one piece. Among them was the skeleton of a complete saber-toothed cat with its paws intact. Laboratory researchers saw with surprise that the inside claw sheath (the one in the same position as a human thumb) would indeed have held an enormous claw. But the claw sheaths rapidly got smaller as they moved to the outside of the foot, toward where the human hand has a little finger.

This meant that all the saber-toothed cat skeletons in the museum had been put together incorrectly! Instead of having one large claw sheath on each foot, all the skeletons were mounted with a large claw sheath on each toe. So, jokes paleontologist Shelley Cox, the specimens on exhibit "are all thumbs."

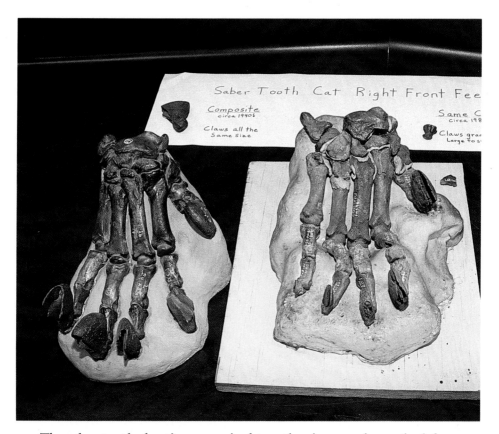

The saber-toothed cat's paw—wired together incorrectly on the left and correctly on the right

Painting the Past

A section of the La Brea mural

The fossilized bones at the Page Museum are fascinating. But sometimes museum visitors have a hard time imagining the animals to which the bones once belonged. This is why the work of paleoartists such as Mark Hallett is invaluable.

Paleoartists specialize in recreating prehistoric environments, people, and animals in paintings and sculptures. In 1988 Mark Hallett created a 4½-foot by 8-foot wall painting, showing an entrapment episode as it might have taken place at La Brea more than 10,000 years ago.

Hallett starts his work by reading "everything I can lay my hands on relating to the [ancient] animals." He also talks to paleontologists and biologists to get their insight on how the animals may have moved or behaved. When possible, he travels to museums that have fossils of the animals he is going to illustrate. He makes dozens of detailed sketches of the skeletons and studies the marks where muscles were once attached to the bones.

Hallett cannot tell everything about an ancient animal's appearance from its bones and muscles though. Some features remain a mystery. Ears and noses, for instance, are made of soft tissue called cartilage, which is not preserved by asphalt. Another feature that remains unknown is the color of the ancient animal's skin, feathers, or fur.

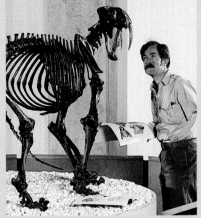

To fill in these blanks, Hallett studies modern animals that are similar to the ancient animals or those that live in similar environments. Then he makes educated guesses about the appearance of the animals that lived in the past. In the La Brea mural, for example, he included an extinct horse. Its closest modern relative was the quagga, a zebralike animal from South Africa that is also now extinct. Like a zebra, the quagga had black-and-white stripes on its forequarters. But the rest of its body was reddish brown. Hallett thought that the horse at La Brea probably had a similar color and stripe pattern. That's how he painted it.

To recreate the prehistoric area around Hancock Park, Hallett studied the plants that left seeds, cones, and wood fragments in the asphalt. He went to the top of some of the tall buildings around the park and took pictures of the encircling mountains.

When Hallett was satisfied with his knowledge of the animals and the environment he was going to recreate, he made a master drawing and copied it onto a piece of artist's linen for painting. Hallett's painting of an entrapment episode at La Brea has been part of a traveling exhibit and is now on permanent display at the Page Museum.

The Pleistocene Environment

In addition to giving paleontologists an idea of how extinct animals once lived and what they looked like, fossils can also tell scientists about the animals' environment—the landscape and plant life that surrounded them. One way to find out what kinds of environments ancient animals inhabited is to study their modern relatives. For example, the ancient rodents found in the tar pits most likely lived in the same kind of environment as modern rodents. So, since small rodents are found in wooded areas today, scientists believe that there must have been woods near the tar pits more than 10,000 years ago.

Some of the large animals found at La Brea, such as deer, llamas, and mastodons, also probably lived in wooded areas. But many other large mammals found in the asphalt deposits—like camels, horses, and bison—are native to vast, open spaces. So scientists think that both woods and open plains must have been present in southern California during the Pleistocene.

Fossils can also provide information about climate, the typical weather conditions found in a region. Animals such as bison, elephants, and wolves live in many different climates and are often able to survive with a wide range of temperatures, foods, and water supplies. So the discovery of a bison fossil at La Brea wouldn't necessarily tell scientists whether the region was hot, mild, or cold; wet or dry. But the discovery of a certain snail fossil, on the other hand, might prove that La Brea was once cold and wet—because that is the only kind of climate in which the snail could survive.

Plant fossils also give clues about climate. The remains of trees such as pine, cypress, oak, juniper, and coast live oak show that there were a variety of climates around La Brea—since pine and cypress live in moist, cool environments, while coast live oak and juniper are from drier regions. Some plant remains would have fallen directly into the asphalt seeps, while others—from different types of environments—perhaps washed downstream from the mountains and hills nearby.

But some researchers doubt that so many different trees and plants existed near La Brea all at once. The wide variety of plant and animal life found in the tar pits leads many scientists to believe that the La Brea climate gradually changed—from moist and cool to dry and warm. Perhaps different kinds of plants and animals came to La Brea in sequence, one after the other, as the climate changed. By looking at the specimens found in each level of the asphalt deposits, paleontologists are gradually developing a clearer picture of the Ice Age environment.

Wetter Weather

Scientists still have many questions about the prehistoric environment and climate of La Brea. But they are sure that for much of the Pleistocene, southern California was much wetter than it is today. They have found the bones of water birds—herons, egrets, swans, and ducks—which need ponds or lakes in which to hunt for food, swim, and raise their young. They have also found large water plants, such as rushes and pond weeds, and microscopic plants called diatoms, which live in springs, lakes, marshes, and shallow ponds.

Fossils of all kinds of water-loving insects have also been uncovered. All of these insects still live today, many in seasonal ponds—the kind that form during the rainy winter and dry up gradually in spring and summer. Other insects found at La Brea would have needed permanent water sources such as lakes or stagnant—unmoving—ponds. Still others needed strongly flowing streams and rivers.

Tiny mollusks (shelled animals) excavated at La Brea are now found only in woodlands far to the north, where rainfall is about 30 inches per year (compared to only about 15 inches for present-day southern California). Since these animals lived at La Brea during the Ice Age, we know that rainfall must have been greater then.

Snail fossils found in the La Brea asphalt show that the Los Angeles area was once colder as well as wetter. The snails survive only in the cold lakes of the surrounding mountains today. Coast redwoods and other cool-weather, moisture-loving trees have also been found. Scientists think that these plants probably grew in the nearby Santa Monica Mountains; their wood and cones washed downstream into the La Brea deposits. But such trees have vanished from southern California and exist now only in the north, indicating that even the mountain climate in southern California has changed.

How They Met Their End

The tar pits were still trapping animals at the end of the Great Ice Age, when mammals such as the mammoth, saber-toothed cat, American lion, and giant ground sloth became extinct. The causes of the extinctions are still hotly debated. But one factor was certainly a rapid rise in average temperatures—of about 10° F. Such a temperature change would have been enough to cause a massive drought that would kill animals and plants.

The flat asphalt deposit found when the Page Museum was built contains evidence indicating that the change in climate, from cool and moist to hot and dry, may have come fairly quickly. This shallow deposit appears to have been a seasonal pond, filled by rainfall, where animals came to drink. As we learned in chapter 3, the pond was probably not the site of an asphalt seep, but most likely filled with asphalt that drained in from elsewhere.

Why did Glossotherium harlani, *the giant sloth, disappear at the end of the Ice Age?*

The lower part of the deposit contained the remains of several very young horses and only one adult. Although young animals were more frequently trapped in asphalt than were adults, paleontologist Eric Scott believes that the young horses may have died due to drought rather than entrapment. During a drought, very young mammals often die at water sources. Their undernourished mothers usually cannot produce enough milk for them, and they are too young to eat anything else. They drink water, but because it doesn't give them any nourishment, they weaken and die. Older animals are still able to travel, find sources of food, and survive. Scott believes this theory might explain why there are so few adult horse bones in the Page Museum deposit.

The deposit offers further clues about how the animals might have died. In other La Brea deposits, bones have been torn apart by scavengers and mixed up by the movement of asphalt. In the Page Museum deposit, excavators found semiarticulated (partially intact) skeletons of a saber-toothed cat and a dire wolf. The wolf was face up, lying on its back. The cat was over it, face down. Researcher George Jefferson thinks the animals may have died fighting each other. He also believes their struggle may have taken place in the thick mud of the drying pond. If they were mired and buried quickly, their remains would have been protected from scavengers and left to fossilize intact.

Eric Scott, however, thinks the animals might have been undisturbed because of drought. During a drought, animals die by the hundreds; scavengers have more than enough to eat. They cannot eat everything and may not fight over bones. Many skeletons are left intact. This theory, too, might account for the skeletons in this deposit.

Scientists still don't fully understand why so many large animals became extinct at the end of the Great Ice Age. One group of creatures, however, did not become extinct during the Pleistocene and continues living today: humans.

CHAPTER
5

HUMANS COME TO THE TAR PITS

A change in climate is the most likely villain in the disappearance of many of the plants and animals of the Pleistocene. But another factor may have contributed to the extinction of North American animals such as the saber-toothed cat, mammoth, giant ground sloth, and mastodon: overhunting by human beings.

The extinctions occurred between 10,000 and 11,000 years ago. Although humans might have been living in southern California at that time, the oldest human remains in the area date back only 9,000 years. Those remains were found at La Brea.

Scientists have very little information about these early Californians. Archaeologists, scientists who study human cultures of the past, base much of what they know about these people on the culture of two more recent Native American

The extinct American lion (Felis atrox)

groups, the Chumash and the Gabrielinos. These two groups, who were living in California when the Spanish arrived, are believed to have descended from the early Californians.

Earliest Uses of Asphalt

Most of the earliest people in California settled near the coast, where food and water were plentiful all year long. They built plank boats and fished the waters between the mainland and the Channel Islands offshore. To seal the cracks between the planks in their boats, they used asphalt.

In fact, the early Californians used asphalt in almost all aspects of their daily lives. They used hot pebbles to melt it, then they spread it on the inside of baskets to make watertight containers. Asphalt was also used to repair broken tools, hold knife blades in knife handles, and attach fishhooks to fishing lines.

At first the native Californians probably used asphalt that had washed up on the beach. This asphalt came from oil seeping up to the ocean floor off the California coast. But it was not long before early people discovered the huge asphalt reserves of La Brea.

Archaeologists are not sure how the coastal people acquired their asphalt from La Brea. They may have traveled inland to camp for a short time near the tar pits and mine the asphalt themselves. Or they simply might have traded with another group of people living permanently at La Brea. Paleontologists discovered the site of a prehistoric village near what is now Hancock Park in 1914. There they found artifacts left by the early inhabitants.

Ancient Artifacts

Only about 100 artifacts have been found. Although they are few in number, the artifacts add much to our knowledge of prehistoric life around the tar pits. Projectile points such as arrowheads show that the early people hunted. They made new arrowheads as they needed them, by using the point of a deer antler (also found in one of the deposits) to flake stone into a sharp blade.

Arrows were used to hunt small animals. But archaeologists have also found an atlatl, or spear thrower, in the asphalt. This device, used to give more speed and power to a thrown spear, indicates that in addition to hunting small animals, the early Californians used spears to hunt large animals.

Some scientists think the atlatl is an indication that early North American peoples might have hunted Ice Age animals like the giant ground sloth. But many paleontologists, including Eric Scott, are not convinced. Scott points out that although the human artifacts were found in the same deposit as the bones of ancient animals, they were not necessarily found at the same level. The tools and bones were likely buried by the asphalt many years apart. In fact, carbon 14 dating has shown that the atlatl is only 4,500 years old. Ground sloths and many other large mammals disappeared about 10,000 years ago.

Other artifacts found in the asphalt include grinding stones, called metates and manos, and even some jewelry: abalone shell pendants and deer-bone hairpins. Most artifacts, however, had to do with the recovery of asphalt. There were wedges—triangular pieces of antler used to dig semihard asphalt—and shovels made out of shells—probably used to scoop asphalt out of depressions.

A Grave in the Asphalt

Much of the daily life of the early Californians is still a mystery. However, the people of La Brea left scientists with an even more puzzling mystery: La Brea Woman.

In 1914 paleontologists digging in Pit 10 found 17 bones from the skeleton of a woman. She was 4 feet, 8 inches tall and about

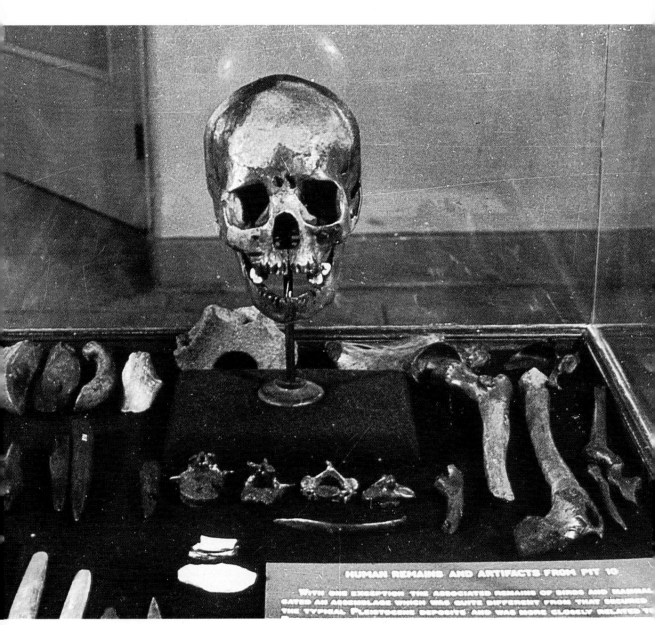

La Brea Woman's skull and bones

18 years old when she died 9,000 years ago. Paleontologists estimated her age based on the wear on her teeth and the fact that her shoulder and hip bones were not quite fully grown.

The skull of the skeleton, which came to be called La Brea Woman, was broken in three places, and the left jaw was fractured. Scientists are not sure what caused the injuries. The young woman could have died from a blow to the skull; she might have been injured in a fall or killed by another person. The damage may even have been done when the woman was buried or when the skull was excavated.

No one is certain how La Brea Woman got into the asphalt deposit in Pit 10 either. Although early paleontologists thought she might have been killed, she was not put there by a murderer to conceal her body, says paleontologist Scott. Asphalt seeps are usually only 2 to 4 inches deep. Nor do paleontologists think La Brea Woman was buried or deposited in the asphalt deliberately. Some scientists suspect that an asphalt seep started after the woman was buried and that oil gradually penetrated her grave.

Grave goods, personal possessions buried with a body, were also found in the deposit. One of these items was a mano that appears to have been carefully notched on one edge. Some scientists believe that the mano was deliberately defaced, or damaged, as was the burial custom of the later Chumash. This clue would indicate that La Brea Woman was given a ritual burial by her people, says George Jefferson.

But if she was buried ritually, he asks, why are most of her bones missing? Not only that, later Chumash buried their dead in cemeteries. If La Brea woman was an ancestor of the Chumash, why was she not buried in a cemetery with the rest of her people?

Christopher Shaw cites research done by Richard Reynolds, indicating that the young woman might have died far from La

Brea and might have been buried temporarily. Later, when they could, her people returned, recovered her body, and buried her at La Brea. Shaw explains that the early people may have been afraid of the woman's ghost and were anxious to get away from the grave as quickly as possible. As a result, they only recovered her skull and 16 major bones.

La Brea Woman's bones are the only human remains found in the asphalt deposits in Hancock Park and the oldest human bones ever found in southern California, Shaw says. Questions about who she was, how she died, and how her bones ended up where they did are sure to remain unanswered for a long while—perhaps forever.

The Asphalt Business

Descendants of La Brea Woman's people were still using the asphalt deposits when the Spaniards arrived in California in the 1700s. As more Europeans settled in the region, they too began to use the deposits.

In the early 1800s, the newly independent country of Mexico governed southern California, including Los Angeles and Rancho La Brea. Asphalt from the tar pits was just as important to the citizens of Los Angeles as it had been to the early Native Americans. Mexican citizens in and around Los Angeles used asphalt for fuel and to make their roofs watertight. At that time, asphalt was considered a community resource. When the mayor of Los Angeles gave possession of the Rancho La Brea land to Antonio José Rocha, part of the agreement was that Rocha would let the people of Los Angeles collect as much asphalt as they needed for personal use.

By 1870 California had become part of the United States, and much of the land around the tar pits was owned by Henry

Henry Hancock was more interested in selling asphalt than in looking for the bones inside it.

Hancock. To Hancock, asphalt mining was a profitable business. He hired Chinese laborers to mine the deposits and sold the unprocessed asphalt for four to five dollars per ton. It was used by local residents to waterproof their roofs and by local businesses as fuel. Hancock also processed the asphalt to remove dirt and bones. In 1875 visiting geologist William Denton described the procedure: "The material was conveyed to large open boilers, in which [the asphalt] was boiled for twenty-four hours, and then run into sand molds; subsequently it was broken up...carted nine miles [to the port of Los Angeles] and shipped to San Francisco, where it was sold for twenty dollars a ton for making pavement." The processed asphalt was also used to seal pipes and to preserve railroad ties.

One remnant of this business can still be seen in Hancock Park. The Lake Pit, where the sculpture of the Columbian mammoth appears to scream in terror, was once the site of a 19th-century asphalt mine.

Although asphalt is still used to pave streets, for the most part it no longer comes from natural deposits. Modern paving asphalt is produced when petroleum is broken down into a wide variety of products such as gasoline, kerosene, and heating oil. Because they come from petroleum, which is originally formed from the remains of ancient plants and animals, we call these products "fossil fuels."

Today the La Brea Tar Pits' principal products are entertainment and scientific information. Each year thousands of visitors play in Hancock Park, look into the black pool of the Lake Pit, and gaze at the coffee-colored skeletons in the Page Museum. Behind the glass window of the Page's laboratory, volunteers and scientists work piecing together this unique collection of fossils and the fascinating stories they have to tell.

The End of the Story?

The asphalt seeps of La Brea have been flowing for 40,000 years. Although there are no mammoths or saber-toothed cats to be

A rabbit caught in the tar at La Brea

Visitors come from all over the world to see the bones at the George C. Page Museum.

snared anymore, squirrels and opossums sometimes wander into the fenced excavation areas and die in the asphalt.

Humans, too, can get stuck. In Hancock Park, Frisbee players may be surprised to find themselves glued to the grass by a small puddle of tar. Paleontologists who work in the deposits every day are the most likely to get caught. Eric Scott got trapped when he stepped into an asphalt deposit to pull out a sign that had been thrown over the enclosing fence. Reporters and other visitors, such as television producer David Attenborough, have also had to be tugged out of the tar. These victims of the asphalt are not usually left there to fossilize, although their shoes or gloves may stay behind.

Even when the last fossils are taken out of Pit 91, the La Brea story will not be finished. Scientists continue to examine the fossils on the shelves at the George C. Page Museum and continue to ask questions. Was it drought that killed the huge Ice Age mammals? Where did the bison go when they left La Brea? How did La Brea Woman die? What other secrets are hidden among the millions of bones? Only time and persistent paleontologists will tell.

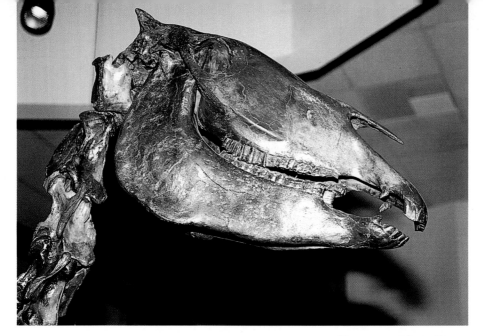

Equus occidentalis

Glossary

archaeologists—scientists who study human cultures of the past

artifact—an object, often handmade, representing a particular culture or human activity

asphalt—the sticky black substance left when certain hydrocarbons in petroleum evaporate

asphalt seep—an area where petroleum has leaked to the earth's surface

carbon—an element found in living things and in substances like coal and charcoal. The carbon in living things sometimes turns into petroleum after organisms die.

carbon 14—an element found in all living things; also called radioactive carbon. Scientists measure carbon 14 to determine the age of fossils.

carnivore—a meat-eating animal

climate—the typical weather found in a certain region on earth

DNA (deoxyribonucleic acid)—a material found in living cells that determines an organism's hereditary traits

drought—a period of little or no rainfall

entrapment episode—an event that starts with the trapping of an herbivore in asphalt and ends when the last scavenger has left the site

excavation—the process of digging, as of fossils; the site where digging takes place

extinct—no longer existing on earth, such as certain animal and plant species

fossil—a trace or remnant of a plant or animal that lived during the distant past

geologists—scientists who study the history of the earth, especially as recorded in rocks

glacier—a large sheet of ice moving slowly over land

herbivore—a plant-eating animal

hydrocarbon—substances, such as gasoline and kerosene, made up primarily of hydrogen and carbon

ice age—one of many periods in the earth's history when temperatures were low and large areas of the planet were covered with ice

mammals—animals, such as humans, elephants, and horses, that nourish their young with milk

matrix—the material in which something, such as a fossil, is embedded

mineral—a nonliving substance such as such as stone, salt, or sand

Miocene epoch—a period in earth's history that occurred between about 25 million and 5 million years ago

organic—made up of or containing carbon. All living things are organic.

organism—a plant or animal

paleoartists—artists who make paintings or sculptures showing plants, animals, and people of prehistoric times

paleontologists—scientists who study fossils to learn about life in the distant past

petroleum—also called oil. A dark liquid, often used for fuel, formed under the surface of the earth

plankton—tiny organisms, both plants and animals, that live in water

Pleistocene epoch—a period in the earth's history that occurred between about 1.7 million and 10,000 years ago

predator—an animal that hunts and eats other animals

prehistoric—existing before written history

prey—an animal that is hunted and eaten by other animals

scavenger—an animal that eats carrion, or dead animals

sediment—particles of sand and soil that settle to the bottom of bodies of water

sedimentary rock—rock formed from sediment

species—a group of animals or plants that have common characteristics and are capable of interbreeding

Index

Acknowledgements Photographs and illustrations used with permission of the George C. Page Museum, pp. 2, 3, 15, 24, 32, 33, 40, 43, 57, 62, 66; James P. Rowan, p. 6; © 1993 Noella Ballenger, pp. 7, 21, 23, 29, 30, 34, 37, 42, 44, 49, 59, 67, 68, 70; *Texas Highways* magazine, p. 8; © 1993 Jalien Tulley, pp. 9, 39, 51; Deneb Karentz; p. 10; Mark Hallett, pp. 16, 19, 52; D. B. Siniff, University of Minnesota, p. 17; Maryland Office of Tourism Development, p. 22; Save Orcutt Community Inc., p. 27 (left); Marian Mullin Hancock Charitable Trust, pp. 27 (right), 65; Trans. no. 4948(4), Photo by Denis Finnin, Department of Library Services, American Museum of Natural History, p. 47; Stephen McBrady, p. 53.

Front cover: Mark Hallett, bottom; Noella Ballenger, top
Back cover: Noella Ballenger